8 Affinities
Jaap Pieters & John Porter

Edited by Chris Kennedy

The idea for this book first came together a few years ago on the train platform in Osnabruck, Germany. The Dutch filmmaker Pim Zwier and I were sitting on a bench after the European Media Arts Festival, waiting for our trains to take us to our separate destinations. To while away the time, we took to discussing the Dutch and Canadian film scenes. He began telling me about the super 8 filmmaker Jaap Pieters and his description automatically made me think of Toronto's own John Porter. Something about the way they worked only in super 8, always traveled with their films and attended practically all the film events in their respective cities seemed like an instant connection. The fact that Jaap, like John, was also a photographer and collector clinched it for me. I thought it would be worthwhile to get them together at some point for a conversation and record it—the results of which form the majority of this small book.

Jaap and John had already discovered their common interests a few years earlier. John toured Europe in 2007 and met Jaap in Amsterdam, where they reportedly had an hours-long conversation in a bar after John's show.

So this second meeting, brought about by the Media City Film Festival in Windsor bringing Jaap to Canada in the spring of 2011, was a chance for the two to reconnect and expand on their previous conversation, this time with a sound recorder running.

My basic interest in this project was the idea that two artists in two separate scenes would have natural affinities, working in similar ways and with particular priorities, despite having no knowledge of the other. The fact that they both worked in a rare medium like super 8, insisted on showing the work on film, insisted on being there to project it themselves and often would narrate their work live (rec room style)—either during projection or after—were the obvious links. But additional links— that they were amateur archivists with large collections, that they would document things with photography (John documents the film scene, Jaap documents his archive itself) that they would attend film events constantly, and that they seemed to be struggling with order and chaos in their films, and perhaps their lives—were equally compelling to me. We see ourselves as unique entities, so the idea that we may have a mirror in another city has always been fascinating—and disturbing—to me. Our culture privileges unique inspiration and originary moments, so two artists working through similar patterns and ideas disrupt that common assumption. Essentially, how do ideas develop in parallel and in isolation?

Of course, as the conversation shows, Jaap and John do not confirm to the rigid taxonomy that Pim and I put them in during that brief moment on the train platform—both of us only knew one of them at that point and were just taken with the idea that they could be twin spirits. Even in the affinities they do share, there is a wealth of difference in aesthetic approaches, personal beliefs and organizational strategies. Their films are arguably only similar in that they share recognizable structures that many super 8 filmmakers use—most notably confining most of their films to the run-time of a single three-minute cartridge. Otherwise there is as much difference between the two filmmakers as between any other pair. However, the conversation also reveals why people have wanted to introduce them to each other with the assumption that they would enjoy a few hours together. What follows is documentation of one of those hours.

– Chris Kennedy

Jaap Pieters and John Porter
in Conversation
June 7, 2011
Toronto

John Porter

I was thinking that because it's been so long since Jaap's seen my films but I saw his just last night, we could talk more about his films than my films. But, then there are general things you might want to talk about.

Chris Kennedy

The general things are in some ways more my interest. When I first heard about Jaap, I thought that there is a lot of affinity between the two of you in many different ways: your collecting habits, your documenting habits and such. I thought it would be interesting to have you guys chat about various subjects. We can be specific about some films, but we can just also chat.

John Porter

Yeah, we share some similarities. But I was interested in the differences too, and I sort of touched on those in the question and answer period last night, like distribution and prints versus originals and 35mm. I'm very interested in how differently you're approaching that whole side of it. And I'm really interested in the whole distribution issue because I've forever had a problem with the Canadian Filmmakers Distribution Centre here where they won't distribute original super 8 films, which is what I make. So they don't have any super 8 since 1989, when you could make prints in Toronto easily.

Jaap Pieters
Well, with me, the whole thing about originals goes back to another, a lot of other levels, and that is my collecting. I mean, when I had specific records that I loved, I always considered taping them and not playing the record. That's a similar thing. It was always like keeping the things as pure and clean, as unused, as possible.

John Porter
You would make a recording, a tape, so you could listen to that?

Jaap Pieters
Yeah, then I thought this LP is so beautiful and it's so special, it's so dear, I don't want to play it even.

John Porter
You don't want to hear it.

Jaap Pieters
I wanted to hear it. I would put it on the tape and then listen to the tape. It's this preserving in its most cleanest, clearest form... I tend to do that extremely. Even all the letters that I write, first I started making photocopies. Then as I started writing them in different colours and writing all these drops or flames on as the dots of the i's,

then I started colour copying them even before I would send them off. It's just the accumulation of everything I gather that almost cannot leave the house.

John Porter
Yeah. Well another thing that I think about—worry about the older I get is—what's going to happen to all this stuff when I die? Do you think about that?

Jaap Pieters
Yeah, yeah. Sure, sure. But, somehow I feel I have time enough to find a solution.

John Porter
You can't count on that. You could get run over by a bus tomorrow!

Jaap Pieters
I know, I know. I don't count on anything, but there's just some kind of gut feeling you have about—some things can be done later—and of course you're always caught in the crossfire and then it's gone. I mean, Fassbinder's writing a script for this film about Rosa Luxemburg, which I would have loved to see, but then, yeah, it was never made.

John Porter
So with your films you make a print right away? And never show your original, generally.

Jaap Pieters
No. I've never done that. There were a few exceptions. I had once two shows in Athens and then I just couldn't find my copies. I had left them somewhere after a show in a house of a friend. I had called him even and he didn't see them. But they were in his place. So, I'd been looking

for 20 hours for those prints…

John Porter
I know the feeling.

Jaap Pieters
And I could not find them and in the end I just took out all the originals and went on the plane, without no sleep and total insanity and…

John Porter
Yeah, if you're like me, I'm like, "I can't wait until I leave town so I can rest". Most people think about a working trip, you know, a tour as work, but once you get on the plane you can rest.

Chris Kennedy
But you tend to show your originals, though.

John Porter
Yeah, I insist on showing my originals. I refuse to make prints. Although I have made prints back when it was easy and cheap in Toronto. You could do it. I tried it and there were a few films that I could tell were popular—that were going to get shown a lot—so I made prints of those. But I would still prefer to show the original. A print I would use if I were sending the film off to some festival where you don't know what the projector is and who the projection-ist is and it's a real gamble. Do you send your prints off without yourself?

Jaap Pieters
No. I never did try to get into festivals. Very early on I did send some. I had a few tapes—somebody made a few tapes for me—and I did send it to maybe four or five festi-

vals and there was never any reply. so...

John Porter
 And you don't get your tape back.

Jaap Pieters
No, no tape back, no answer. No nothing.

John Porter
And you paid an entrance fee?

Jaap Pieters
No, no, I never did that.

John Porter
Yeah, I don't enter festivals, either, partly because I don't
like the entry fees, but I don't have prints. I don't even
have preview video copies.

Jaap Pieters
Yeah, so I had a couple and I don't know where they are.

John Porter
But I'm not interested in showing my films at some festival on the other side of the world where I'm not there to
enjoy the audience looking at my films, you know. I don't
get any reward from that.

Chris Kennedy
You both tend to show your work as a whole show and
you're usually there providing a narrative. Do you want to
talk about that? Why do you choose to do that?

John Porter
Well, I'm there anyway, because I'm showing my originals

and I like to oversee the projecting very carefully. In fact doing my own projecting, that's why I asked you at the beginning, "Jaap, are you going to be doing your own projecting?" At that point, I didn't know they were prints.

For originals, I pretty much insist on doing my own projecting and clean the projector thoroughly before I show them and I ask the history of the projector. That's why I wouldn't send my films off to a festival either, because you don't know what the projector is and who the projectionist is.

So I'm there anyway and I'm a talker like you and a performance artist, too. I've done some of that. I like performing and so it just evolved over the years. I just talked between films and I just started talking over the films. And that's why I was interested when you said at the beginning, "Yeah, we can talk between films and you can ask questions, but not during my films." You know, you're very strict about that. The films speak for themselves.

Jaap Pieters

Yeah. The films should talk, I think. To me, they have a language. I never called myself, my films, poetic, but they were called poetic many times. It's not up to me to say that they're poems, but they've been called poems. So in that sense, there is a language in the films that could talk to

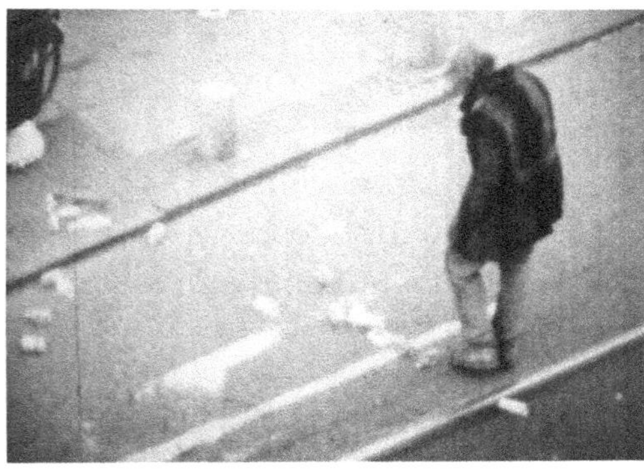

De Blikjesman
(The Tincanman)
Jaap Pieters. 1991

people and I don't want to disturb that.

John Porter

Yeah, definitely there is that. I'm happy to show my films without any commentary, but... Do you remember what you thought about me talking over my films? What did you think?

Jaap Pieters

Yeah. I remember that I liked your show a lot, but it was very different than the way that I do it.

John Porter

Yeah, but what do you remember thinking about me talking over top of my films and allowing the audience to do the same. What did you think about that?

Jaap Pieters

Well, I think it suited your work because there is—and that might be the same in my case—there is not such a specific difference between you and your work. You show a part of yourself...

John Porter

I'm in a lot of my films. Unlike you.

Chris Kennedy

Jaap, you said that after awhile you realized that you were shooting yourself. That your subjects represented you.

Jaap Pieters

Well, that took me years. That really took me years. It took me years to see that. That actually started at this point when some people started calling me the Tincanman. "Oh, you're the Tincanman". The first time it actually happened was 1998 and I had been seeing these Yasujiro Ozu films. I forgot which one. In the Filmmuseum they had a retrospective of a whole month. Thirty-four of his films. I saw thirty-one in that month but I also wanted to see a concert of Pere Ubu. So I went to Pere Ubu and there was this guy standing next to me, he was taping the concert.

He looked at me and he said, *"De Blikjesman. Hello, Tincanman"*.

And I only said, "Well that's not me, but I made him, yes. I made that film, but that's not me".

It seemed later on that he just had moved into the apartment right opposite of my apartment on the same floor, the third floor...

John Porter

The Tincanman did.

Jaap Pieters

No, this guy who had said that. We only found out about that after the concert of Pere Ubu. We both went the same direction and in the end it showed up that he was living opposite of me. He had just moved in there. And that was interesting because he also is somebody who is always— he used to tape everything, always constantly. He had hundreds of cassettes and he did that since he was four- teen and then he had—by being too drunk and too much into all kinds of other things—had set his place on fire, so he lost all his singles and all his tapes. And even the tapes—that was interesting—the tapes were all somehow melted together in a couple of huge blocks and he kept them. He still has them.

And I can relate to that. It almost feels like, they are there for our geologists later on, if ever anybody wants to… That's the thing about when you die. A couple of years ago there was a film journalist who had died and he

was very famous in a certain period and he had an incredible huge collection of everything about film. It actually
was supposed to go to an archive, either the Filmmuseum
or whatever. There was some kind of mistake and they
borrowed a huge container and they threw it all out. And
people passed by and saw all these very valuable things of
the '30s, '40s—film magazine, photos, stills, everything!
And people started dragging out things.

John Porter
Well, I hate to say it, but I can see that happening to your
collection and my collection and a lot of other peoples'
collections. I don't know if you know tENTATIVELY a
cONVENIENCE. He commented about a huge collection of stuff and, oh yeah, he was trying to find homes for
some of his videotapes—his compilation videotapes of
other people's work that he had made. I said, "tENT, what
about all your own work, what's going to happen to that?"
It's all going to end up in the garbage someday.

Jaap Pieters
Well, that's the thing I don't believe but it's a matter of a
certain gut feeling, I think.

John Porter
You need to find somebody younger than you who wants
to preserve it all.

Jaap Pieters
Yeah, yeah. I know a lot of people younger than me.

John Porter
But do they have the incentive, the interest in keeping all
of your stuff? Your huge collection of stuff?

Jaap Pieters

I don't know. I don't know.

Chris Kennedy

Have you made inquiries into people who would be into preserving your work?

John Porter

Not personally, no I haven't asked around about it, but Janine Marchessault—she has been the chair of the film department at York University. She's interviewed me a couple of times, written about me. She said she'd like to get my archives donated to York University which I would really like because Joyce Wieland's archives are there and CEAC's archives (The Center for Experimental Arts and Communication, which was a precursor of The Funnel). So it would be a great place. But, she has to lobby for this and I don't know how actively, how much time she has to spend on that. But I also don't know exactly which archive she's talking about, you know. At the very least, my films, but I think she's also thinking about this huge collection I have of film programme notes and posters from Toronto—all the people have shown over the years. How much of that are they willing to take, because I've got peripheral stuff to, that's not directly related. Well, how much are we talking about? Something to think about.

Jaap Pieters

But I really, I just trust that those things will go right. I've got a really strong feeling. You're known. A lot of people know you, a lot of young people know you. So if you would die, people, several people right away would think, "Oh my God, what about John's stuff? What about John's films?" And they would come into action.

John Porter
You can hope.

Jaap Pieters
For you it's a matter of hope, for me its a matter of trust. I really feel that. Some of my originals are now in the Filmmuseum archive.

John Porter
Yeah, how many?

Jaap Pieters
I dunno exactly, I forgot.

John Porter
About ten? Twenty? Fifty?

Jaap Pieters
No, about twenty.

John Porter
These are original super 8 films? And you've got prints of them?

Jaap Pieters
Yes. As I've said, I've only shown the prints always. But then I think that they even returned to me the originals when they had the first four blown up to 35mm. It was not the Filmmuseum that did it; it was De Filmbank who was then separate from them still. They applied for money and they had some funding come from somewhere. The other two that were blown up to 35mm are certainly in their files. Now we had agreed on doing sixteen more to 35mm. I delivered maybe ten, but I couldn't find them all. My place always was in extreme chaos.

John Porter
Mine too. Have you seen these 35mm blowups?

Jaap Pieters
Yeah, yeah.

John Porter
And how do you like them?

Jaap Pieters
I love them; I think they're really beautiful.

John Porter
Yes, you were saying that they show more detail then you
see in the originals.

Jaap Pieters
Yeah, yeah.

Chris Kennedy
Have you looked into blowing yours up to even just
16mm?

John Porter
I can't remember now, but I did have one or two blown up
to 16mm. Again, when it was easy and cheap to do in Toronto. There was a lab that did that. That would have been
in the early '80s. I wasn't happy with the results—it was
more contrasty; we lost some detail that way. And it was
expensive and I couldn't show it easily because I didn't
have a 16mm projector.

Jaap Pieters
Yeah, yeah. I always thought, I'm not going to change anything because I don't have a projector. I don't even know

how to handle this projector and I was never interested.

John Porter
So I gather from what I asked you last night at the show that you didn't even know whether these 35mm blow-ups were being shown. You're not notified of any screenings…

Jaap Pieters
Yeah, but that's probably…

John Porter
Do you get a paycheque or something that would give you some indication that they were shown? But in any case they're not being shown with you there unlike all of your other films.

Jaap Pieters
Yeah, sure.

John Porter
So they have a different life.

Jaap Pieters
Yeah, yeah, yeah, yeah. But with the 35mms I don't care so much. Somehow they're so different from me that I don't care anymore.

Chris Kennedy
Why don't we open this up to the question: "Why super 8?"

John Porter
Oh yeah, this is the question I get all the time from audiences: "Why super 8?"

Jaap Pieters

Why super 8? Well, for me and super 8... I was taken to the cinema by a friend a couple times and then I really got hooked on cinema. I had discovered a couple of filmmakers myself. The first one I discovered was Ingmar Bergman. I was growing up in a town where they had two cinemas, but there was nothing more than the usual porn in that period and then a few blockbusters. That was about it. So, Ingmar Bergman you would never see there. Then they were suddenly shown—I think it was '72; I was around seventeen— on television. This was the first time that I felt, "Oh, wow, a film is made by somebody. It's not the actors that make the film; somebody is making this film."

And then the second retrospective or series they had on television was by Pasolini, and that was the second one I discovered. And that really blew my mind. *Uccellacci e uccellini* was... inCREDible, I didn't really... Whoa, this was such a different dimension.

John Porter

Can I ask how old you were?

Jaap Pieters

Seventeen. Around. I might have been sixteen. I remember the house of our neighbors. It was not in our own place, my own home. It was in the house of the neighbors and they were watching these films, my parents didn't. About sixteen or seventeen. Around that age.

And then after that: pretty soon came Fassbinder and Wim Wenders. And then I discovered cinema when I ended up in Amsterdam. Then I was already twenty-two and so then I just dived into the cinema and always tried to watch it as much as possible.

I had friends in Germany who were really extremely politically involved and they were shooting super 8. That was around '79, '80, when I met them. I went to their screenings, which was a 600-kilometre hitchhike just to see their screenings. But I just did it.

John Porter
What city were they in?

Jaap Pieters
Kiel. Kiel. It's on the East Sea. It was an important marine harbor city. The first part of the German revolution in 1918 started in Kiel.

Chris Kennedy
Who were these friends?

John Porter
Someone we would know?

Jaap Pieters
They had certain collective called Chaos.

John Porter
Oh! K-A-O-S

Jaap Pieters
No, no. C-H-A-O-S. I became friends with them. The three guys that were mainly at that point Chaos was Karsten Kaplan, Karsten Weber and Henning Jansen. And I hung out a lot with Karsten Kaplan at first. He was doing his civil duty because he didn't want to go into the army, so he had to do another job. They had this collage film of three hours—one film—on super 8. All copied, all printed.

John Porter
When you say "collage", was it original footage that they had shot?

Jaap Pieters
They shot everything themselves and they edited it all themselves and they added music to it and it was a typical product of the seventies, I think. The end of the seventies I think they shot it. I was really, really moved by that. That you could combine political activism with filmmaking on that level. On this more or less collage level. And apparently because I asked them a lot of questions about the films at one point a guy just sent me a film camera. "Go film yourself. Go shoot yourself." Wrapped up in a pullover, in a plastic bag. Just sent off to me.

John Porter
What about film stock?

Jaap Pieters
Well I could buy that, of course. Most of the shops still had film—mainly AGFA was cheaper—so I started shooting on AGFA. As you can see in the portrait of Willem.

John Porter
Did you have to send it back to Germany to get it processed?

Jaap Pieters
It was done in Arnhem still and I brought it directly to the photo shop and they took care of it, with all the other photo material. But then I noticed that these political things were not directly my thing to do myself. I'd been trying a lot of things, different things, and I had huge, really huge things in my head.

There's a lot of footage that I shot of the tearing down of the house that I used to live in. I had some kind of party, a dinner for my family, my parents and my brothers and sister and had organized that in my old house. The funny thing is halfway through the film or halfway through dinner a part of the wall came down. Ha, ha. It's really an amazing moment.

But it was all just trying, you know. I had borrowed a couple of cameras. At that point I had three and there were two guys filming that party. A third of it is almost black, a third of it is totally out of focus and one third was, well, kind of okay. And I had ideas for editing it together, mixing it with the footage that I intended to shoot myself of the tearing down of the house, which I filmed but I never came to editing.

Until the moment that I just grabbed the camera because I didn't believe what I saw. When I saw the Tincanman. That was the first big moment. and I still didn't feel like showing it. I mean, people really said, "Oh, you must show that." My father said, you must send it to the VPRO, which is a broadcasting foundation. The amount of broadcasting time was based on their amount of members, a very Dutch system...

John Porter
But getting back to why super 8. At that point, did you ever try 16mm?

Jaap Pieters
No, no, no.

John Porter
And why not? Why did you decide well this format—super 8—this film format is for me?

Jaap Pieters
Because that was the level on which I understood it. It's a camera you can take in your own hand. There's not too many buttons. It's just the simplicity. You don't have to think much about it, you can shoot directly.

John Porter
Yeah.

Jaap Pieters
Of course I've thought a lot about it and at first I thought so much about it that it never came to anything.

John Porter
A few years ago I saw a screening at the National Film Board of super 8 films by blind people. Of course they had help, guidance—a sighted person. The way he talked about why he chose super 8 for this project was just fascinating to me because it opened even my eyes more about how simple super 8 is compared to video. As you say, on video cameras you've got all these menus and buttons. You've got to be able to see. With super 8, you can feel it and each dial has different feel than the others.

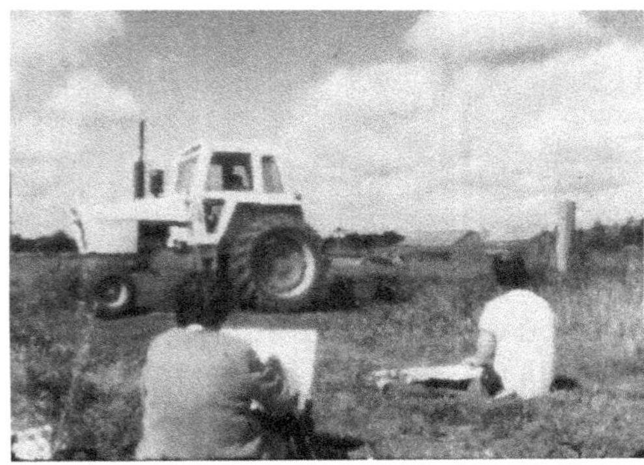

Landscape
John Porter. 1977

Jaap Pieters

Yeah, that would drive me nuts: all those buttons.

Chris Kennedy

Was that the same for you, John? Was that why you got into super 8?

John Porter

Yeah, there were some similarities, but I started out in still photography…

Jaap Pieters

That was another… but go on first. But that was another thing that I started with as well, actually.

John Porter

So I was getting photography magazines and in one of them, there was a column talking about how your home movies don't have to be just a document of your family on vacation or a birthday party. You can write a little story and do a little enactment. I thought, "Wow, never thought of that before."

So I rented a super 8 camera and wrote a little narrative and got my friends out into the vacant lot nearby, with costumes and props and things like that and shot. As soon as I started shooting this film, I thought, "Oh, this is for me! Moving photographs. This is what I want to do."

I was already an amateur actor—not performance art. Yeah, it incorporated acting and narrative and photography. So then I decided, "Oh, I'm going to go to film school". I was already thinking that I was going to go to photography school. It's the same school here in Toronto: Ryerson. So, by the time I got to Ryerson I was more interested in film.

It was all 16mm there. No super 8. They were like,

"Seriously, if you shoot a film on super 8 we're not looking at it, we're not marking it." You know: that sort of attitude. It was training people for the industry. And the main thing I learned about school was how much I didn't like 16mm because it was so expensive and complicated and fragile. The equipment. You know, one little thing goes wrong and it costs $100 to get it fixed. And crews to shoot, even if it's one other person. If you have sound, all of a sudden you need one other person with a Nagra recorder. Just so much more cumbersome and bothersome.

So I was at Ryerson and then I started seeing experimental films at Ryerson, too. They were showing Michael Snow and Stan Brakhage and so I got the idea, "Well, I want to make films that are so simple that I can do everything, direct, act, edit, sound, project." And that was super 8.

Jaap Pieters
Another thing which you have mentioned is that these schools train people for the industry and they always had. I always had a very strong sense of resisting this society on that level. Now I can analyze more or less why, but back then it was only a real gut feeling. "I don't want to live in this world."

I was very, very influenced around… I think I was twelve or thirteen and I saw this footage of Auschwitz. I saw all these things that were filmed in the concentration camps and that really, really, struck me that deep.

John Porter
There was that French film that was around a lot then: *Night and Fog*?

Jaap Pieters
Yeah, yeah. I did not see it but, yeah.

John Porter
I forgot the director... Alain Resnais.

Jaap Pieters
And Vietnam was going on. So I saw a lot of that on
television as well. So that was the point for me. "I don't
want to be a part of this world. This world is too awful to
be part of." I was very politically motivated and I realized
super 8, to me, is not a thing that "they" make money with
anymore.

John Porter
Well, I also saw super 8 as a political statement, just
choosing to shoot in super 8. I partly got that from Ryerson where they looked down on super 8. They looked at
it as inferior and I always liked fighting for the underdog.
"I'm going to prove these guys wrong. I'm going to make
super 8 films that are just as good as theirs, try and show
that it can be a fine art form". Maybe even more so than
the larger film formats because it's more like a paintbrush
or a poet's pen.

    That, to me, wasn't necessarily "not being a part of
the world", it's more like fighting that world from within.
It was a very confrontational position I took. I think I'm
pretty confrontational anyway, that's part of my character,
but I'm still doing that. I still find that after all the work
I've done and other people have done and despite people
coming out to screenings like yours, generally there's still
this attitude from the film people that super 8 is inferior.
It's not real filmmaking.

Jaap Pieters
Well not so much anymore...

John Porter
Well I think it's still very dominant.

Jaap Pieters
Yeah, but…

John Porter
In fact when you get people asking you, "Why super 8?" That comes from that. They can't figure out, "Well why would someone choose to work in super 8?" It just doesn't make sense to most people.

Jaap Pieters
Well, I don't get that question so much. I know that at a certain point maybe ten years ago that it was used way more by artists and video makers that really wanted this typical kind of grain—this typical grain in their films; in their projects; in their art.

John Porter
The super 8 look.

Jaap Pieters
Yeah. That was picked up by people in advertisements…

John Porter
It still is in music videos…

Jaap Pieters
And that had a huge influence on a lot of several huge feature films.

John Porter
Yeah, but that's something different. They're not using super 8 the way you and I are. It's sort of just a tool for a

larger purpose, which is making these big commercial films.

Jaap Pieters

But not for the artist. I mean I know a guy who lives from making commercials for television, but he's a huge fan of super 8 and he always shoots everything himself on super 8. Of course, for a commercial you cannot shoot everything on super 8, but as soon as he can somehow use super 8 within the commercial that they have, he does.

John Porter

But it always ends up getting transferred to video or to digital or at least blown up to 16mm. And that's another reason that I like projecting on film. And even more so, projecting originals. Because it's more radical. It's something very few people do and its sort of a political statement. It's also why I like talking over my films because I don't see anybody else doing that so I like to think its radical. "This is radical, man, talking over my film. Nobody else is doing this. Nobody else is showing their original super 8s. You know, I'll show these people you can do it".

Chris Kennedy

So, it's about the setting in many ways. You're creating the cinema as you perform it.

Jaap Pieters

Yeah, but what I don't fully understand is being radical for the sake of being radical.

John Porter

Well no, it's for the sake of showing how super 8 can be a radical medium. It's not some just home movie thing that amateurs use. That you just show to your friends.

Jaap Pieters

Yeah, but it was. The home movie thing—that has disappeared, of course...

John Porter

But still, super 8 is still couched in those terms by people talking about it. Non-super 8 filmmakers talking about, "Oh, it gives it that home movie look. Remember that old format your parents used to shoot home movies on?" That's how they see super 8.

Jaap Pieters

Maybe. That might be different in Canada than in the Netherlands, in Europe.

John Porter

Well, I wouldn't be surprised.

Jaap Pieters

That might be different here.

John Porter

Canada's very conservative and we see Holland as much more liberal, even radical.

Chris Kennedy

So you don't identify with the word "amateur" in relationship to what you do?

John Porter

Well, no, yeah. I do, partly.

Chris Kennedy

What is it about that word that you identify with?

John Porter

Well the fact that you can't make much money at it, but also the films I'm making look like—some of them look like amateur films. There's nothing sort of avant-garde about them. Just straight documents of things, you know, they're like a home movie. No, I embrace all the terms: "home movie" and "amateur".

Jaap Pieters

Well, the whole idea of amateur is a thing that I like because that to me is also a political statement. Dividing people up in their profession, their personal life. That's all actually, at the moment, a matter of politics.

John Porter

It depends what the amateur is doing, though, because there is this whole international community of amateur filmmakers. They're probably all on digital now but they used to work in super 8 and 16mm when I was getting to know them in the '70s, '80s. They're usually doctors, lawyers, teachers—people who make a living at something else. They are weekend filmmakers and they'll just make little dramas and documentaries and they're very conventional in their structure. As I say, a lot of them would be working in super 8. But then you get amateurs more like you and I, who aren't making just those types of films. What makes us amateurs is we're not making money out of it. It's a much more artistic approach to the format.

Jaap Pieters

Yeah, but for me, I never cared about all these terms. I mean, you can call me an amateur, you can call me whatever, I don't care. I've never called myself an artist. I don't give a fuck about the whole system, those systems. It's all those systems!

John Porter

Yeah, that's the difference for me because I mind the system and I like to call myself an artist in order to give super 8 that respectability.

Jaap Pieters

Yeah, but then you have more of a mission than I have. That sounds a bit like having a mission. I don't have a mission.

John Porter

I do.

Jaap Pieters

I am my own mission, probably. I mean I've really had to fight for my position to exist because I always felt that I could not exist in this world. There was no place for me in this world and I never wanted a regular job. I never wanted, actually, any kind of job because I absolutely felt totally alienated in all those little worlds in all those little systems. Fred Pelon shot his video project about me that I should not forget to send you a copy. In there, we talk a lot about super 8 and at a certain point he asks me, "Well, is it not just some kind of religion?" Well, no, it's not a religion. It's about something else.

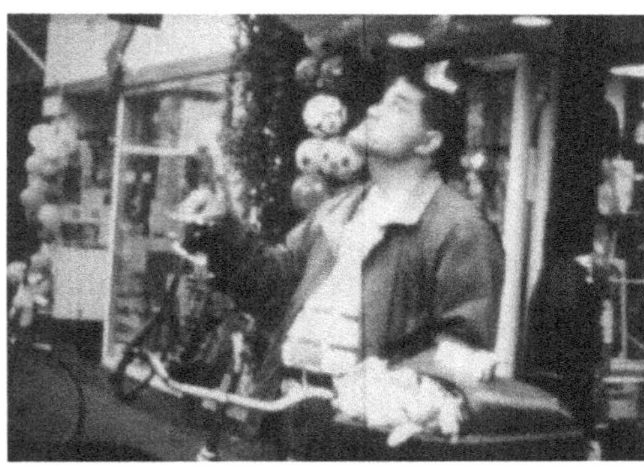

De vliegenier
(The Flyer)
Jaap Pieters. 1995

Only in the explanation of the word *religare*, as "becoming One". In that sense you might call my decision of shooting on super 8 a religious one. Or of my approach to super 8 as a religious move. Because to me it feels like it is part of everything that I am and that to me is important. It's more like, here I feel at home. This is a thing I can deal with.

Two years ago somebody asked me, "could you register this whole art opening of a huge project for me on video and I'll pay you 100 euros?" Well I needed the money so I was walking around with this stupid camera for four hours. But it's so confusing. I mean, you are there, but you are not there. Constantly you see the little screen where you see only this part of what's around you. Really filming, keeping the camera directly to your eye would be so different.

Chris Kennedy
What is that about, then, with super 8? When you say you're there with the camera?

Jaap Pieters
Somehow the camera protects me against the outer world that I never feel that I really can be a part of and it also connects me. So it has these both things. Filming the homeless people for me started at the point where there was, on another level, a change coming up for me as well.

The first seven years I lived in Amsterdam, I had about two hundred different people in my house. I think most of them I just met on the street. They were not homeless people. They were mostly young people traveling. They would always ask me, "Would you know a place where we can spend the night? Would you know a cheap hotel?"

I would say, "Yeah, come to me." I would cook for

them. I would buy them drinks. I would show them the city. I did that for seven years.

But at a certain point I noticed that I don't have a filter. So everything always goes totally in. Into me. And so every time when they left I was there, quite confused, extremely lonely. I didn't know what to do with myself. And at one point I decided I don't want these people in my house anymore. I've been giving and giving and giving constantly all that energy. It's not about the food or about the money. It's about this attention. I needed that for myself to feel that I had a right to exist because in this society I never felt that I had the right to exist. But with them, guiding them through the city and feeding them and giving them a bed, I felt that I had the right to exist.

That stopped because I just couldn't take it anymore. Some of them are still good friends. Those people from Kiel—those Chaos people—I met in that way, on the street. I met three guys while I was hitchhiking and they were from Kiel. They met their friends in Amsterdam, somewhere on the street and they took them to my place as well. So I was thinking I would have three guys in my home, but when I returned home, there was seven.

But then, by having this camera, I noticed that I can participate in that world but not be fully absorbed by it. That gave me another way of existing without really losing myself in those other people.

But I recognize—and that took me a really long time—that I've only been filming myself. I am the "Tincanman". I am the "Trolleyman". I am all these people. This is how I travel. When I travel I always travel with way more than I would ever need. Piles of paper. The last maybe ten years I've paid a little more attention to my clothes and I always take too many shirts, because I can't decide.

John Porter

Now when you're describing what you do to a complete
lay person who's never seen anything of yours or maybe
never seen any super 8 films, how do you describe it? Do
you have a term? There's all these terms I don't like, like
"experimental". Often I find myself saying, "Well a lot of
people describe my films as experimental, but I don't like
that term". I prefer the term "personal".

I was just thinking about that now when you were
talking about how all these films of other people are actually about you. In my case I'm actually in my films, so in
a literal sense it sounds like both your films and mine are
very personal films.

Jaap Pieters

Yeah, yeah.

John Porter

Like you said, you didn't like the term amateur vs. professional. But do you have some term that you will sometimes use, maybe reluctantly, just to describe what you do
to somebody who has never seen your work?

Jaap Pieters

Well, when people ask me what do you do: "Well I make
short movies, on super 8". I always say I make short movies. First, I make film, short films, super 8. And then they
say, well, what are your themes: "Well, I don't really have a
theme."

John Porter

What are they about?

Jaap Pieters

Yeah, What are they about? So, "Well, my program is

mostly built up out of a series of portraits I did with homeless people. It's their act of being, their way of being, and there's no sound, there's no explanation and it's mostly shot on one roll."

John Porter
Do you ever use the term documentary to describe what you do?

Jaap Pieters
No. No. I think it is not documentary at all. People have been calling them observations, which I like. But then I always add to that that is only a part of the program. The other half of my program are films of a simple movement caused by a machine or a person or the wind or anything that moves me. I try to frame it in a way that it is only about that movement. I call them my abstract movies because they get a certain sense of abstraction by the way I frame them. But actually they are not abstract at all because they are extremely concrete. The only abstract thing is that people don't understand what they see and why it is moving and what it actually is.

But it is not about what it is; it is about what it does to me. It's about the movement. It is some kind of sheet draped over a field where they have sown some kind of plants to keep away the frost, but I try to keep that out. Because that is not what I see, no? That's important for me. That is not what I see. I don't see the "why and what". I see only what is hidden inside or behind or in the movements themselves.

John Porter
None of my films are abstract, but I like using that term when I'm explaining to these lay people because often when you say, "short movies", they're thinking of short

movies they see on television—short dramas like that. So then I say, "Well, they're sort of documentary like home movies," and then they start thinking about documentaries they've seen.

It's really hard to get them thinking about what you're really doing and I find, "Well, think about the idea of abstract film." And that really jars them, they don't know what you're talking about and they have to really use their imagination to think, "Oh, abstract film, that's not documentary; that's not anything that I've ever seen on television." It's a good term, I think, to get people thinking about what I call "personal filmmaking."

Jaap Pieters

What I usually end with when I describe this first part as the homeless, the second part as the abstract. I then say my preference is to show them mixed, because in the end they are not about these homeless people or these abstractions; they are about seeing. They are about the way I perceive the world. I see the world like that.

John Porter

Yes. And that's what all art is. It is really artists showing what they see that other people aren't seeing. You're sharing your vision with other people.

Jaap Pieters

On that level I might accept the term "artist" for myself. But you really have to define it first quite well.

Another interesting thing about what you said... This book was published, *Square Millimeter*, about Dutch experimental film. You know that book?

John Porter

No.

Jaap Pieters
Erwin didn't show it to you? It's called Dutch experimental filmmaking between 1960 and, well, 2004. And there
are 120 filmmakers with a filmography in it. It was published in 2004 and I had told about it to friends in Switzerland and they wanted copies.

John Porter
Are you in it?

Jaap Pieters
Yeah, yeah there's an interview with me in it as well. I had
planned to bring two boxes because I thought, "I always
sell a few." It was all too complicated and I didn't have
time to pick them up from the Filmbank. They're really
beautiful books there's a lot of photographs out of the
films in them.
        Then this one guy in Switzerland asked, "Oh Jaap,
do you consider yourself being experimental?"
        "No, I don't care, but if they ask me for an interview in a book and they call me 'experimental' I say yes. If
they would call me something different, I would say yes. I
don't care what they call me."
        You know, and now, suddenly they have decided
that my films are experimental. Okay, that's up to them. I
don't care.

Chris Kennedy
It seems that you, John, have a different relationship to
the camera than he does. You are working with the idea of
what the camera can do and how you can perform with it.

John Porter
Yeah. I'm a bit of a scientist. I'm sort of exploring what the
camera can do. Different things the camera can do. So, I'm

trying different, a lot of different things.

Chris Kennedy
So you are kicking the tires and trying to get a sense of
what the camera does?

John Porter
Yeah. And a lot of times that's the main incentive for
making the film. What would happen if I did this? What
would this film look like if I use this function on this
camera in this way that hasn't been done before? I've gotta
see that! I gotta see what that looks like. So yeah, it's a real
sense of discovery.

Jaap Pieters
Yeah, yeah. I remember that in your work. That's an ap-
proach that I really like, but I wouldn't be able to do it.
Not that its necessary, but I like that in your work.

John Porter
Well, you're discovering things, too, for yourself, when
you shoot those films of those people.

Jaap Pieters
Yeah.

John Porter
When you look at it, you're seeing something that maybe
you weren't seeing or thinking of when you were shooting?

Jaap Pieters
Yeah, I was.

John Porter

Most of my films have people in them and in that sense it's very similar to your whole collection. I have a few sort of still life films and I always like to semi-joke when I'm talking, "I like my films when they're funny." I like making funny films. I find that as long as you have people in your films, they're going to be funny, no matter what. How do you feel about that? You may not use the term funny, but I think you were talking last night about the entertainment value or something like that.

Jaap Pieters

This is funny, actually, what you tell now. This is funny.

I had done a screening once in Bern, Switzerland and there were seventy people and there was no reaction, nothing. Nobody said a thing to me. They chattered away with each other and they left. And then, they had me walking to the place where I was staying with the projector, with the bag of films in the rain. That was a difficult night.

I also had done a show in Basel, where there were only two people. They came with such personal expectations, feelings and reactions that I always gave these two shows as an example that I'd rather have two people that are really interested and moved. Two guys that I've never

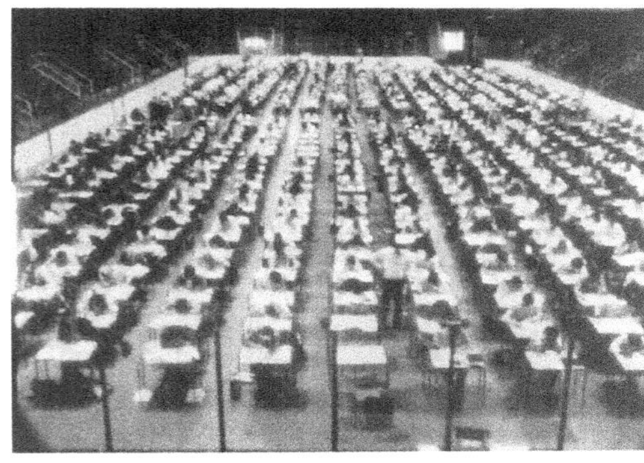

Exams
John Porter. 1982

seen before that are really moved by my films is way more important than seventy that don't react.

Then a couple of years later the same guy who organized that first tour in 2000 tried to organize a second tour in 2004. He called them up again in Bern and then they said, "Oh no, we don't want that guy anymore. His films are not funny."

So they should have taken you.

John Porter
Yeah.

Jaap Pieters
I'll tell them next time.

John Porter
Do you have some sort of policy or feeling about including people—the essentialness of people—in your subjects, in your films?

Jaap Pieters
Well, maybe when I look back at them I can see that, but not while shooting. I never think while I'm shooting. I really have to be hit here somewhere. When this feeling is there then I shoot.

Chris Kennedy
For you, John, you often set things up. For example, you would set a timer to capture a condensed ritual. It seems like your films are premeditated.

John Porter
Yeah. I'm planning my composition, my subject and my location in advance. I'm planning my compositions actually days before I shoot. Yeah. I do some improvising, but... I think you were talking last night about chance and

accidents, often in the stories you were telling. Its actually in your films and I guess partly with mine, too. But the stories make the films even more enjoyable; hearing what happened before and afterwards and all these coincidental things happening—like that lady coming in and stomping out the fire and the little girl sort of making a face at the camera, you know. They always seem to be at just the right time—the dramatic climax, you know, two thirds of the way through the film.

I often say in my talk that I think, unlike all the other art media, photography and cinematography have this opportunity for chances and accidents to happening and you should encourage that. I find that often, maybe even more often, such films are more interesting than films that are so planned—you know, scripts and budgets and re-shoots and all that stuff. Its much easier just to let the subject make the film and it will be just as good if not better.

Chris Kennedy

Continuing with this idea of chance: Jaap, it seems that a lot of your work features someone amongst the disorder—a character surrounded by a world that is disorderly. For example, *Jimmy's Ballet*, where he's trying to control the traffic. And John, there are elements of that with your stuff, too, where you're in the center of the frame and the world is spinning around you.

But there's also a way that your work seems to order chaos in some ways. When you have a condensed ritual, you kind of see the systems that people walk through, the order that people become. So I wonder if you guys think about order and chaos in relationship to the street scenes that you shoot and the world that you shoot.

John Porter
 Well I think chaos is beautiful, that's why I film it.

Jaap Pieters
I think it's the main source of all creativity. I think it's really the most important thing there is. Chaos.
	But my films are mostly quite empty and there always is a lot of space in the framing. If you would see my photography—it almost only exists on contact sheets—it's always extremely chaotic. It's always extremely full, just like my apartment always was. I need this chaos around me, and only to have a lot of chaos around me, I find some kind of rest. People have tried to convince me for years and years and years that I would be way more at ease with myself if I would have a more clear environment.
	They don't get it and its sometimes quite tiring to always have to explain to them that you really need this total mess in order to have some kind of clearance in your head and that while I'm chaotic in my head it's not because of that mess, it's because of too much pressure.

John Porter
Yeah. There are these new TV shows, like *Hoarders*, about people who hoard stuff. But these are like reality shows where they always bring somebody in to help them to get their place organized. There was a recent CBC show done by this funny CBC reporter, Josh—I forget his name—and he's apparently one of these hoarders, too. He was interviewing people who were happy with their chaos. There was this one guy he was a federal cabinet minister and the solicitor general. He was the head judge or police guy in the country. His office was just total chaos, but he knew where everything was. This guy was just loving it and doing one of the most important jobs in the world with his chaotic life.

Chris Kennedy
That's a good segue into your collections. You both collect a lot of things. Do you have particular collections? What do you collect?

John Porter
Well, there's different collections within my collection, but some of the things I collect, a lot of people collect, like books and magazines. But I'm practical minded, so I like to stick to small things. That's why I like super 8. It's so small and practical. You can collect a whole bunch of equipment: cameras and projectors, and they don't take up that much space. I also collect miniature toys and after many years I decided to make a super 8 film about it. That turned out quite well, so it partly justified that huge collection of toys.

Jaap Pieters
But do you need this justification?

John Porter
Yeah, well I did. I felt that I had all these toys and what purpose were they serving?

Jaap Pieters
Yeah, but why do they have to have a purpose?

John Porter
Well because they're taking up space. The joy was in the purchase of them. A lot of collectors are like that, right? You buy… obtaining it. And then you put it away and you never see it again, you know. It doesn't make sense, so I said, "Oh, I should make a film of it and then I will document them, at least, and then I can see those toys when I look at the film."

Jaap Pieters
Does it have to have a sense?

John Porter
Yeah, I guess, part of me thinks that because I am practical minded. I had sort of an interesting upbringing. My mother has been an artist, a painter and a very eccentric sort of crazy mentality whereas my father was a scientist, a physicist, very practical and efficient. So I'm coming from both those sides. I think it shows in my films, too. So a side of me says, you know, there has to be a reason. Always I have to make use of it. It has to have a purpose in my life.

Jaap Pieters
Yeah, but that's my struggle with people. People always say, as soon as you haven't touched it for ten years, you can throw it away.

John Porter
Yeah, that's what they say, these organizers, these professional organizers.

Jaap Pieters
So, it's not about that! It's totally not about that! It's not about use of the things, it's about it existing. It is there. And that gives it the right to exist. Maybe that comes, I never realized that, from what I said before that I always felt that there was no place for me in the world. I did not have the right to exist. These things have no right to exist but they're important to me. Maybe on a certain level there's some kind of identification.

  I love packages.

John Porter
Packages.

Jaap Pieters
As soon as they're empty, they are interesting to me. I don't know why.

John Porter
Oh, they have to be empty. Because then they're only a package.

Jaap Pieters
Yeah. I think I never threw away any of my film packages.

John Porter
Yeah.

Jaap Pieters
So, I don't know how many...

John Porter
Actually, I noticed you were talking about envelopes.

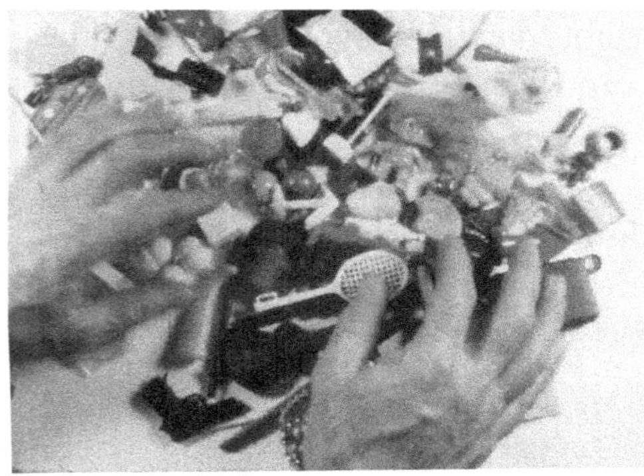

Toy Catalogue 3
John Porter. 1996

Jaap Pieters
Yeah, yeah. I'm obsessed by envelopes.

John Porter
For me they're boxes. We always got them back in a box,
a cardboard box. The super 8 films. You got them back in
envelopes?

Jaap Pieters
Envelopes.

John Porter
Well, I've saved all my boxes, too, because, actually, they're
a practical way of storing the films because they stack easily. That's not the same with envelopes, though.

Jaap Pieters
No. No, but I mean, I always kept the boxes in which you
buy them.

John Porter
Yeah.

Jaap Pieters
I don't think I've ever thrown any away.

John Porter
Yeah. I used to go to Exclusive Film Lab and behind the
counter I'd see a garbage pail and they'd be full of these
cardboard boxes and I'd be, "Oh, can I have a few of
those?"

Jaap Pieters
Well, there was one point, I remember, because I never
threw out any of the plastic filmcans…

John Porter
Yeah, me neither.

Jaap Pieters
But there was one point where I had this friend who did
a lot of photography and he always would roll black and
white film into cassettes.

John Porter
Yeah.

Jaap Pieters
And he had planned to go to Indonesia, and he said,
"Yeah, the problem is, with the Kodak filmcans, they're
actually too thin." He thought, "The Fuji you can see
through," and he didn't trust that. And he saw these Agfa;
they were black.

John Porter
Black, yeah.

Jaap Pieters
And thick.
And he said, "Could I have a few?"
"Well how many do you want?"
"Well, if you would have ten?"
"Well you can have fifty. I don't care."
He said, "Whoa fif-"
I said, "Well you can have a hundred, I don't care. I don't
need them and then they have a purpose."
And that goes beyond me and then I can help somebody
with that. And, then it's absolutely no problem to give
them away. The fact that within a year, he committed
suicide and his brother probably threw them all out, that's
another thing.

John Porter

Well, there you go again. You die and even your brother is going to throw everything out of yours. But part of the reasons I keep a lot of this stuff is for ecological reasons. I tell this in my *Toy Catalogue* film, I collect pieces of plastic, like film cans, to keep them out of the landfill. But then a few years ago you could put them in the recycling box, so I got rid of a lot of my plastic film cans then.

Jaap Pieters

Really?

John Porter

But, there are varieties of them. I kept a collection of all the different kinds of film cans, you know, brown ones, ones with a round top and super 8 cans, too. And regular 8 cans, there's a very interesting variety of those. And reels, super 8 reels. An interesting variety. From Kodak you used to get the reels—grey or something in the blue or black plastic one-sided can.

Jaap Pieters

Yeah I remember those, yeah.

John Porter

Those are precious to me, because you don't get those any more.

Jaap Pieters

Yeah, I remember those.

John Porter

And they protect the reel from being crushed or something in transit.

Jaap Pieters

Well, that is an other side, of course. It's this whole historical thing. The development of a certain product. And I've always been interested in that on many levels.

John Porter

Yeah, me too. I have another interest in history. Local history like Toronto history. The history of film. The history of super 8.

Jaap Pieters

That's probably a big difference. That with you, you have these specified...

John Porter

Purposes...

Jaap Pieters

Well, subjects.

John Porter

Yeah.

Jaap Pieters

Super 8 is a subject. Toronto is a subject. As for me, everything always goes everywhere. I mean, suddenly I notice, okay I have ten different phone books laying around. I'll never use them; they use up a lot of space. I could throw them out. But then, "Oh, wait a minute. Each year has a different front cover." So, I tore them all off. Well, this has a certain historical development and that is really interesting. It goes like that, I think.

John Porter

Things we've been talking about now just make me think...

we were talking about home movies and originals and history, what about this whole home movie scene. Have you ever obtained or collected other people's home movies?

Jaap Pieters
Well I kept them at the point that they were given to me and then I kept them. But I never really collected them.

John Porter
This is one reason why I'm worried about my own collection, because I've collected home movies too and you'll find a family's whole collection of home movies. Like a document of their life thrown out or being sold at a yard sale and usually it's because they don't have a working projector. They can't see them and the people who shot them die and the children aren't that interested and I think that's what's going to happen to my films.

Jaap Pieters
No, no, no there's a huge difference. You're well known all over the world in a specific circle, but you're known and that makes a huge difference.

John Porter
No, but I don't think it's any different than the children of the parents who shot these home movies. The children are in these home movies. They should be just as important to them as my films are to these people you're talking about.

Jaap Pieters
No, no, it's really different. I think it's very, very, very different. A lot of people are not interested in their own past.

John Porter
Yeah, you're right.

Jaap Pieters
The people who are interested in your films value them as
a piece of art. They like you as a person. There are many
different levels that I think people really define your work
totally different than anything else.

John Porter
Well I agree with you that very few people are interested
in their own history and I find that frustrating.

Jaap Pieters
Yeah, yeah, okay but that says more about you than them
or the world. I mean if everybody would remain interested in his own background, in his own history and
everybody would keep everything, this world would
have been way too full already with storage and archives.
Internationally, that is already such a huge problem at the
moment. All the archives don't know where to store their
things. They don't know how to categorize these things.

John Porter
Yeah, and they are falling apart and trying to figure out
how to preserve what they got let alone collect more.

Chris Kennedy
Well in terms of history, I don't know as much about Jaap
but John, you've been documenting the film scene here for
quite a while.

John Porter
Yeah.

Chris Kennedy
And Jaap, were you photographing the film scene as it
happened?

Jaap Pieters
No.

John Porter
See that's again a mission of mine. Because again I see this whole super 8 scene and even the so-called experimental, avant-garde personal scene as being so fragile that I wanted to document that history in Toronto, at least. Just to do a little bit to keep it from disappearing someday. At which point, yeah, nobody will preserve my films because the whole scene's just sort of dissipated because there's no history of it.

Chris Kennedy
Jaap, your photography is different?

Jaap Pieters
Well I've always been taking photographs for a long time wherever I went. I mean recently I saw a whole bunch of photographs that fell out of a box and I wouldn't recognize any one of them and they're all in my apartment.
    And I'm, "Jesus, oh, looks like a German girl and a guy who might be her boyfriend. I don't know."
    I didn't ever write down any names or anything. Maybe if I would really study on the whole thing. That always is interesting to me. You had those time capsules that Warhol had several ideas about and so every box to me is a time capsule. So without knowing who those persons are, I can somehow trace back to the restaurant receipt or the Cinematheque ticket and maybe even a hand written address that's in the same box from what period is what and who might have been there. But, that is not really consistent because the boxes fall apart and some things have to be repackaged.
    That is actually quite a big problem for me at the

moment. With everything I've always collected because it
is too much. I've collected always everything, every wrapper, every whatever, every ticket. Everything, I've never
thrown away anything. And that is a problem. And if I
just keep it the way it is then it will be a problem for my
brothers if they were to follow. I'm the eldest of five and
they are not interested. I know that. They are not interested in that part.

       They're very aware of the importance of my films.
My youngest brother Marc, for instance, he always says,
"Yeah well I can get you in touch with this or that person,
he's an American guy and he's very good at organizing."
Not organizing my life or my home but my film screen-
ings and really getting money out of it because I'm always
without money and I can't deal with money. It's disastrous.
It always has been extremely disastrous. Me and money.

Chris Kennedy
And John, do you photograph outside of documentation?

John Porter
No. All of my photographs are pretty much of filmmakers.
Sometimes maybe some family shots that document some
historic occasion, like relatives visiting from outside the
country or something.

Jaap Pieters
Maybe that is also the difference between us. Your more
scientifical approach to a lot of things gives you the possibility of dividing and seeing that this is part of that so that
is not part of this. With me, everything that comes my
way is part of me. So, I might have documented important
moments just because I was there, but I never divided
it up as an important moment Like two people meeting
each other: a Russian filmmaker and a Chinese filmmaker,

whatever. I was aware that it was happening and I was aware of the importance, but that next movement back in my home, back in my house, that pile of paper was as important. People really have to go through everything, in my case, if they want to find somewhere something of importance.

John Porter
Another interesting thing about my choice of shooting photographs is, as I say, its sort of a mission to sort of document the history of this community and the reason I'm doing that is because nobody else is doing that. If I don't do this it's going to get lost. So often if I see somebody else taking photographs at a screening I won't bother. Oh, somebody else is documenting this. I don't need to. And I may not even know who that person is or if anybody's going to see those photographs. I don't care. At least somebody's documenting it.

Jaap Pieters
I know that feeling very well, but at the same time if your collection has to be complete you should do it as well.

John Porter
Well it can never be complete. That's impossible.

Jaap Pieters
Well, as complete as possible.

John Porter
Well, it's endless...

Jaap Pieters
That's interesting because here I am being the scientific person. Because I recognize what you said before about

your father and your mother. My mother didn't paint or anything, she was a mother and a housewife, but a very emotional person. She was so heart warming that if you get too close to her you might get burned. But she would never throw away anything. So after she died, any drawer you would open, everything would be spit in your face, all kinds of newspaper things and she would just collect and collect endlessly as my father would never collect anything. He was a mathematics teacher.

John Porter
Oh yeah, that's similar to my parents.

Jaap Pieters
But he also taught bookkeeping and science and chemistry. And he was obsessed by languages and was always studying the grammar of a language.

John Porter
What happened to all of your mother's stuff?

Jaap Pieters
It's mainly still there in the house.

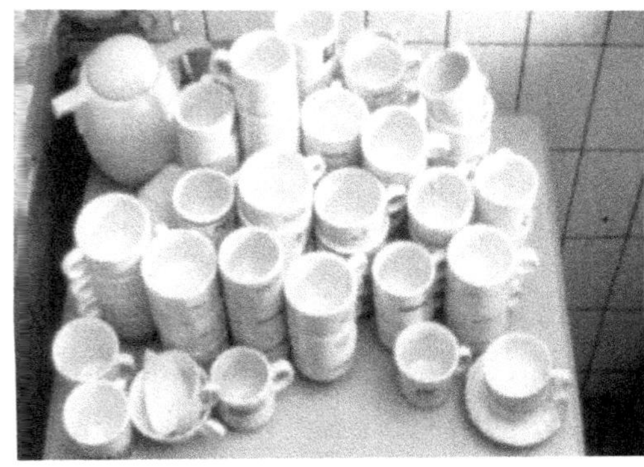

*Des Kopjesdans
(The Cupsdance)*
Jaap Pieters. 1994

John Porter
Her house?

Jaap Pieters
Yeah, Yeah,

John Porter
Is she still alive?

Jaap Pieters
No, no. She died two and a half years ago.

John Porter
Who is living in the house?

Jaap Pieters
No one. It's crazy. It's a museum.

John Porter
A mother museum.

Jaap Pieters
Motherly museum. That's a good one! Well, it's a bit
complicated. I've got only one sister who lives in the town
where we all grew up, where my mother still lived. So my
brother-in-law has always tried to get the things organized
and try to sell the house. Because I don't care and my
other brothers don't care enough, apparently. So he has
been taking out things out of the house that I absolutely
didn't agree with, but I didn't want any more tension as
there already is.
            My parents moved into that house in, I think, '72.
But I never really lived in that house. So they just stored
all my stuff in that small bedroom that they had reserved
for me. But it was all just put there. And it's still there.

John Porter
Do you have stuff that you value in that room?

Jaap Pieters
Yes.

John Porter
Films?

Jaap Pieters
No, it was before I was ... 900 LPs.

John Porter
Oh, yeah, wow.

Jaap Pieters
That's still there and I have no place for them in Amsterdam. There's no space.

Chris Kennedy
Well what's your relationship to music for both of you?

John Porter
Music? Not very much. I'm not musical and I don't really put music on my films. Actually, you know, I have a very strong feeling about putting music to films. I think it's a real crutch. Especially when it's loud music or very dramatic music. It really dominates the film.

Jaap Pieters
So what did you think of that film of mine yesterday. *Willem I, Willem II, Willem III*. The Portrait of Willem.

John Porter
Um. It had music?

Chris Kennedy
It started silent and then…

John Porter
Oh yeah, you played it twice.

Jaap Pieters
Yes.

John Porter
Well, the music made the film more entertaining but I
didn't need it. I didn't hear the question and answer about
that, but he was listening to that music?

Jaap Pieters
Yup, yeah.

John Porter
So I made that assumption when I was watching it silent.
I was happy with that. The film was more about his movement, which I thought was fascinating. Yeah, the music
wasn't necessary but I enjoyed hearing the music just like
we do when we're in a bar.

Jaap Pieters
But, seeing it twice then. That was not necessary for you?

John Porter
Well, I like the idea of showing the same film twice under
different circumstances. People have done that before.
That's sort of a concept that's used in avant-garde film.

Jaap Pieters
Yeah, we could say that showing it twice under different
circumstances is partly what the film is about. It partly is

about you see an image and there is no sound and you see exactly the same image with sound and the same image changes completely.

John Porter

I don't know. At least as interesting to me was seeing the same film over again regardless of whether there was music or not. "Oh, I'm seeing this again. I get a second look at this part here."

Jaap Pieters

Yeah, yeah, yeah. That's very interesting because that never comes up in questions and answers. That never comes up. When something is said about it it is mostly, "Why do I have to look at it twice? I've seen it already." A lot of people get the difference between no sound and with sound.

John Porter

You know if somebody said that to me and they sounded a bit confrontational or upset, I'd say, "Well actually, I think a good film, especially a good short film, you should be able to look at over and over and over again." So if you only want to see that film once you don't like it very much.

Jaap Pieters

That's interesting. There is this American writer Nicholas Carr, who recently published a book called *The Shallow* on how Internet changes people's way of thinking. I mean it even changes brain functions. What his book is about is that everything is brought back to information. Our brain is more and more getting used to the idea that all information has to have a function. The information you gather you only can gather through clear questions. But that's an extremely limited part of the brain that is functioning like that. And that's the reason why I would be very interested in reading that book.

It was just translated recently before I left for Canada. I made ten photocopies of the article. I was thinking of writing letters on it so people would get a letter from Canada with a Dutch newspaper article on the back about that book. I think our way of thinking to a certain depth is exactly not about information. Is exactly not about usefulness. Reducing everything to, "Can I use it? Can I sell it? Is it of any use?" That way of thinking is so extremely limited. All really important discoveries in science on all kinds of levels were always found because there was an endless way of thinking around the thing. They never had a real goal or a purpose. And that's the thing, according to Nicholas Carr, we're going to lose. And that really will change society immensely, I think.

He is somebody who used the internet for a long time and he found that it was almost impossible to get away from it and he wrote several books to really describe the danger of too much use of internet. Because it is forming our brain in one direction. And that I think is really incredible.

And I've always felt that I never really can think in terms of usefulness and maybe that's why I collect everything that's absolutely of no use and that gives them the value. That they have no use. And it's always been a gut feeling that that has an importance. Now books like this being published. You can maybe think more concrete about those different approaches towards life or things and how it affects our brains.

I fell in love with this girl who was 25 and I was about to turn 40. She just turned 25. We had a short affair, but she was extremely practical. She had done this school for becoming a physiotherapist, and then she wanted to study, and she was playing trumpet. And then she started studying philosophy. And she was doubting a lot, "I don't know why I study this." And I kept saying, "I think it's so exciting because it has no use."

She always came back with this question what's the use of philosophy? I think its one of the most important things. I told her, "It's only proven after fifty years what you write now in the end will affect our way of thinking." I mean when it's really original. A lot of philosophers always have somehow tried to grasp in a more scientific way how we approach the things around us. I think that's extremely important.

Even in Japan, I think somewhere in the '70s they decided, you don't need any creativity. You don't need children to learn to draw or to write. Music, it's all not necessary. So in many schools, they skipped all these creative lessons. Until they found 30 years later, people had no creativity. That suddenly was something they were lacking in their companies. People were not used to thinking for themselves, to find creative solutions. They were always extremely good in copying. That's what the whole economy gave it such a boost from in the '50s. Copying the things that were designed in the United States. But, this creative way of thinking, I think it's extremely important for society.

John Porter

It's just starting to come around that way to thinking that way now. Philosophers and economists are thinking that creativity is the most important thing to their economy.

Jaap Pieters

But the ones who are in power at the moment think opposite.

John Porter
Yeah, it's a new way of thinking. Another thing I wanted
to say about music…

Jaap Pieters
Oh, yeah, sure. I always drift away!

John Porter
I agree with the common theory that film is like music—
visual music. The same way its like sculpture. So, in that
sense, that's another reason I don't think it needs to have
music added to it. It is its own music. It's really an interesting medium for that purpose, structuring films like music.
	One time I did try music and this is my condensed
rituals, you know really fast moving documents of people,
crowds and things like that. So I picked out this instru-
mental jazz music by a band called Brand X. It was in the
'70s. Very fast paced. It was perfect. But, I did a show using this music but I played it sooo quietly. As I was saying
that with especially loud music, it just sort of dominates
the film and takes away from the film. So I played the
music so quietly you could barely hear it. And I remember
one guy in the audience yelling, "Turn up the volume!"
	You know I liked that I was sort of bothering peo-
ple, sort of upsetting people. They could hear that there
was music but they could hardly hear it. I never saw that
done before. I've never done it since and I've never seen
other people do it. I still have fond memories of doing
that. Even today it sounds like a really radical idea. Playing the soundtrack so quiet you could hardly hear. You
can just barely tell there is something there. It's a challenge
to the audience.

Chris Kennedy
Jaap, you've shown your work with music. With people

improvising.

Jaap Pieters

Yeah. I've done a series of shows with live music. I don't think my films need it. It's always depending on what people want from you. Last year I was invited for a short tour through northern Spain and the guy who organized that had a musician in mind who's a friend of mine. So I thought it's great to go on tour with Hilary. I love him. He's a very sweet guy, very beautiful. He has a very beautiful approach to music. He plays trombone and electronics and it's very interesting what he does. So, we did fours shows together. I then did two other shows without him and he did two concerts without me.

But it never needs it. That's true. It never needs it, but it has the possibility as well, as long as the music does not blow away the image. That show in the courtyard in Windsor was interesting.

Chris Kennedy

Oh yeah that was great.

Jaap Pieters

Travis, he was a very sweet guy from Chicago. He had seen my films in Detroit and we got along very well. At one point, I said I was invited by Anthology Film Archives in New York in October.

He said, "Oh, well, maybe you could do a show in Chicago then."

I said, "Well I'd love to."

And then he said "Well, maybe, if you feel like, we could do a tour. There are seven cities in between Chicago and New York and I could organize concerts and film shows there."

Well, It would be fantastic. A real North American

tour. And then suddenly he said—because I was still going to do another screening in the courtyard of Media City— he said, "Well your films should not have music, I think."

"Why do you think?"

He said, "Well they don't need music. They don't need music so there shouldn't be any music."

"Well its not that there shouldn't. I've done these things before and…"

"Yeah, well, I brought my guitar."

I mean he was eager to play but he didn't really… it was so sweet, so shy.

John Porter

He was afraid of doing something wrong.

Jaap Pieters

Yeah, yeah. And he was afraid to embarrass me by pro-posing something.

I said, "No, Travis! Bring it out! I mean, ask Jeremy if he agrees but take it out, bring it."

So he took his guitar and he was very excited about it and then there were these, how do you call these?

Chris Kennedy

Wheelbarrows.

Jaap Pieters

Wheelbarrows. There were two wheelbarrows standing there and one stood exactly where I wanted to have the projector and I need this away. So I asked Travis and he said, "Oh! I'm going to need that. I'll take that away for you. I will need that."

And he set it up in front of the screen and he used it in a magnificent way. I thought it was great what he did!

John Porter
As an instrument. As a musical instrument.

Jaap Pieters
Yes, yes. It was all so directly improvised but so much feeling. There is always the risk. Yes, there's always a risk. There's always the risk that somebody really blows away your film, or that the sound gets so much attention. Ute came to me. Ute Aurand—during him performing, during the film—she just came to me, "Oh you should have taped it, you should record this, this is so beautiful".

I thought, "Oh, you don't have to tell me. I know. It's very beautiful but why taping it?"

That was another thing I've been through many times before. People liked a certain concept that much that they wanted me to fix that music straight directly to my film because that is the most perfect thing. No way. Ever. This is the moment now.

Then I always refer to Eric Dolphy on his last studio recording that he did in the Netherlands. On that LP, the last lines he speaks are, "After the music is over, it's gone in the air. You can never capture it again." He says a few lines and I think those are the last few lines he speaks. And they were also, probably, the last recorded lines that

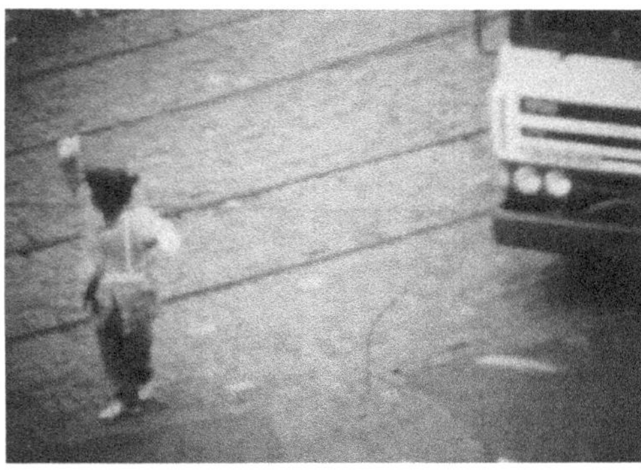

Jimmy's Ballet
Jaap Pieters. 1993

he spoke as this was some weeks before he died.

I have a very strong attachment to music. I've always said before, "My records are more important to me than my films." Because I come more to life with them than through my films. People never understood that but I think it is more because my films are me. So I don't discover much through my own films as I do in music. Music always has been the most important element in my life. That's why the first time I heard *When the Music is Over* by the Doors: "The music is your only friend until the end." That stuck in my brain for a long time. I don't know if I still agree with it but, music is always...

The same as with you, for my first films I was thinking, "Oh, well, what kind of music would it need? What kind of sound would it need?" I tried several things and I always thought, "No, it doesn't fit. No it doesn't fit." Then a German friend of mine wanted to play some mouth harmonica with his favourite film and he was very good at that so I gave him that film *Jimmy's Ballet*. The original. I just gave it to him. "Go on, try."

He came back with a videotape that a friend of him had taped of the film and together they had composed some kind of soundtrack. It was so horrible to me to the film. They just looped several parts of Jimi Hendrix. The guy must have thought, "*Jimmy's Ballet*. Jimi is Jimmy. Jimi Hendrix is Jimmy. Let's add some Jimi Hendrix. Loop it a thousand times. Got all this expensive equipment, loop it and that was the soundtrack..."

John Porter

One thing nice with music on film or with film is that it's temporary. It's not permanent. Especially live music but even music that's married to your print. You can always turn it off.

Jaap Pieters
Yeah, that is true.

John Porter
Aside from that: I made films once with this band in the '80s. Actually, it was their idea. They were super 8 filmmakers themselves and they were renting films from the library and showing them, you know, avant-garde films and showing them behind them. And then when they saw my films, it was their idea. "Oh, John, why don't you show your films with us when were playing?"

Chris Kennedy
This is Fifth Column.

John Porter
Fifth Column. Yeah, they're sort of an all women art college punk band. So I tried showing the films I had shot separately and I found those distracted from the band too much. They were fast paced. "People are just going to be looking at my films they're not going to be watching the band." Then it was my idea to make films specifically for that purpose.

Jaap Pieters
Oh, yeah.

John Porter
A different film for each song. I still don't see bands really doing that today. I was deliberately making the films very minimal. We called them wallpaper films. Just one subject all the way through with very little happening. So that people after they'd seen the film for a few seconds, they realize, this is all it's going to be and they'll go back to looking at the band. It's more background. I really liked

that project. You mentioned touring around. That was
great because bands get more gigs than filmmakers do, so
they're actually touring around, showing in the States and
stuff like that. So at CBGBs, we did a show.

Jaap Pieters
Really? Yeah. Oh wow.

John Porter
Yeah, for a couple of films, I shot synch sound super 8
films. They weren't music. They were sort of ambient or
sound effect sounds like firecrackers going off. I only
made one that we actually showed with the band. I made
two other ones—*Blade Sharpener, Shoveling Snow*—which
were meant for them but were never shown with them.
But that, again, I think it's a really radical idea, which I've
never seen any band do: make a separate film to show
behind them with each song and a sound film! I've never
seen anybody do that. That's a great idea that I never really
explored fully.

Chris Kennedy
One other question: Jaap was talking about Warhol as a
big influence.

John Porter
Warhol.

Chris Kennedy
Yes, and I was wondering about you, John because you've
got the *Porter's Condensed Rituals*.

John Porter
Yeah.

Chris Kennedy
And for me Campbell's cans always have a Warhol impli-
cation. Is there an influence for you for Warhol?

John Porter
Yeah, more the concept. I never really saw *Empire* until,
I guess it was a few years ago, and they didn't show the
whole thing at the AGO. It was a shortened version, clips
or something, right? Remember that? Just the whole concept of it. You know the film *Empire*? *Sleep* and what was
the other one, *Bite* or *Eat* or something like that? Eight
hours. Yeah, just the whole concept really fascinated me.

Chris Kennedy
But naming your condensed rituals after Campbell's soup
cans?

John Porter
Yeah, his soup cans were world famous, yeah, it was sort
of a reference to that when I …

Jaap Pieters
Kind of homage as well?

John Porter
Yeah, I guess the title for the series might have come from
that idea, too, of the soup can. Oh, I should call these
condensed rituals. It sounds like a soup and I can make a
soup can as my poster.

Jaap Pieters
Yeah, yeah. Sounds nice.

John Porter
Porter's Condensed Rituals.

Jaap Pieters
Oh, I saw that in the book!

John Porter
Yeah, and the Porter's looks like Campbell's, I duplicated
the script, font style and made it look like a Campbell's
soup can but it was *Porter's Condensed Rituals*. The picture
was, instead of a bunch of peas—like pea soup—it was all
these people.

Jaap Pieters
Ah, yeah right.

Chris Kennedy
And for you, Jaap, Warhol was a different type of inspiration?

Jaap Pieters
Yeah, yeah, he really influenced me a lot in my thinking.
It was a certain recognition that at some point almost was
a bit scary. To me it started with the Velvet Underground,
hearing that music and on seeing that cover. And that's
the first time I heard of Andy Warhol. On that cover of
that first Velvet Underground LP. That cover was important to me, but it started with the music. The music was
very important.
        I saw the cover and then this name Andy Warhol.
Who is that guy? And then I found a catalogue of his first
big exposition outside of the United States. I think it was
in Sweden. He had his first big solo show exposition and
that catalogue you could buy very cheap in the Netherlands. I saw all these other silk-screens and then I saw
these dollars painted, these cola bottles and they had a
sense of humour. An absurdity, but then I saw his disaster
series, the electric chair which is already a bit shocking at

that point. But then seeing these car accidents, a simple photograph out of a newspaper taken and printed seven times on one canvas. And that really blew my mind. I was shocked. How can you use such a horrible photograph and print it seven times?

John Porter
It becomes a pattern now, like wallpaper.

Jaap Pieters
At that point I realized what he did with photography and actually what he did with press photography. Probably more cruel than the fact that they printed that was the fact that there was a photographer who shot that terrible accident. You see all those bodies around and that it was printed in the newspaper was horrible and they sold it as news. And that made me really think of that whole system of press and reproduction and this whole idea of reproduction. And then I started thinking about that. So there I consider Warhol as a big influence on me. And then watching his films for the first time, they blew my brain out on a different level.

John Porter
When did you get to see them? Like I say I didn't get to see them until recently.

Jaap Pieters
Chelsea Girls I saw.

John Porter
Oh, yeah, *Chelsea Girls*. That was almost mainstream for him.

Jaap Pieters
Yeah, yeah.

John Porter
Well, we showed that at The Funnel in the '80s. Early '80s that's when I saw it first.

Jaap Pieters
I've seen that somewhere early '70s, but I don't remember very much of that. That was the only one that you could see. Then there was another festival that had a couple other of his films in it. Then there was a huge Warhol retrospective in Hamburg, so I traveled up to Hamburg, I traveled to Paris. I traveled everywhere to see those films. Several of his films I've seen five or six times. *Vinyl*, for instance is such an incredible film. And its based on the same book as *Clockwork Orange* is. I mean, the book is called *Clockwork Orange* and the film is called *Vinyl*. And I didn't know about all those things. I just went there. And I started recognizing some of the lines that were used in the film *Clockwork Orange*.

"Jesus," I thought, "Wow, these are the same words that come from the film *Clockwork Orange*." I never read the book. "Oh, wow, this is *Clockwork Orange*. This is Warhol's version of *Clockwork Orange* and that's really…"

I had to go there again the next day to see it once more. He really was a big influence in my thinking and then I started reading so much about him that I really I started recognizing so much that at a certain point it became a bit scary. And I remember I came to my grandmother's birthday once and my mother was sitting there, there was a whole crowd sitting there and I was upset about something, so I was very emotional when I came in and they were all a bit teasing me and then that was the worst that they could do to me. Then I got more upset and more excited and then my sister just, "Calm down, calm down." She touched me.

"Don't touch me, don't touch me."

"Wow," said my aunt, "you're like Andy Warhol. You don't want to be touched."

I said, "No I don't want to be touched."

John Porter
Who said that you're like Andy Warhol?

Jaap Pieters
My aunt.

John Porter
Yeah, she was pretty knowledgeable to know that about him.

Jaap Pieters
Yeah, yeah. I remember that when his stuff got filed. Filed? You call it filed? Sold by auction. We say *geveild*... that's ...

John Porter
Auctioned off...

Jaap Pieters
He had his whole house, five floors, six floors, full. A huge house, lot of rooms on every floor. Everything was packed and a lot of things had never come out of their package. He was obsessed with buying. Just buy for the sake of buying. They found that he had sunglasses, ten of the same one. So if he would like something, he would buy ten right away. And I had done that with records...

John Porter
Is that house in Pittsburgh?

Jaap Pieters
No, that was in New York. And I had done that myself.
I had been buying books that I like so much that I right
away bought five copies. Or an LP or a single. I remember
buying *The Mercy Seat*, by Nick Cave and the Bad Seeds.
I bought 13 copies because 13 was the only suitable figure
to that song called *The Mercy Seat*. I had to buy 13 pieces
so I have 13. I still have them.

John Porter
LPs or 45s?

Jaap Pieters
It was a 45 maxi-single. So it was a large format and it was
a long version. A seven-minute version, I think. I was so
obsessed with it that I had to buy more. And then this
catalogue was published with everything that was in Warhol's house for his auction. And I bought that catalogue. It
was extremely expensive. I didn't want to unwrap it. They
had a beautiful wrapper around it of gold paper. And it's
still there, packed. I never unpacked it.

Chris Kennedy
Is one enough for you, John? When you collect something
is one enough for you?

John Porter
Oh, yeah. Well, except if I'm buying little plastic toys that
are a dollar each. Then I buy a handful.

Jaap Pieters
You would buy more and they would be exactly similar?

The same thing?

John Porter
Yeah.

Jaap Pieters
And what is the reason then?

John Porter
In that case because I like the feel of these toys that I col-lect. They are plastic. I like the feel of plastic and holding them in my hand. When you have a bunch of similar toys, there's more texture, more feel. You can roll them around in your hand.

Jaap Pieters
Yeah, yeah, yeah.

John Porter
Another thing that I wanted to say about music, because you were talking about your early influence—you talked about Bergman and Pasolini and now Warhol. When I was a still photographer and a teenager, I was most in-spired by the Spaghetti Westerns with Clint Eastwood in them. I hadn't seen any foreign films but these were really

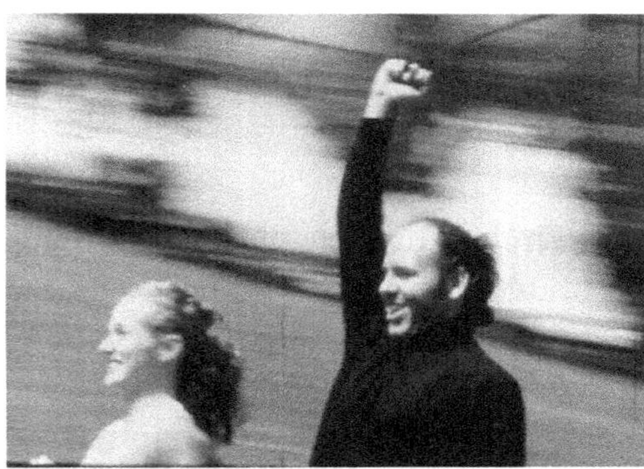

Cinefuge
John Porter. 1974

foreign. They were Spanish-made. Italian-made in Spain. They were so extreme, so stylized visually with this over the top music. It just opened my eyes to at least one of the things that's possible with cinema and I never thought of before. I went to a lot of those foreign films when I was in film school but I didn't get a lot of them. I felt it was almost our duty, like, "Oh, I have to see these films."

Jaap Pieters
Really?

John Porter
Yeah, they're respected, they're written about a lot, but I didn't get a lot of inspiration from them. I was more inspired by Norman MacLaren and Charlie Chaplin and Jacques Tati. I guess he was more of a foreign filmmaker, but... And experimental films. Michael Snow...

Chris Kennedy
You did mention that, in *The Good, the Bad and The Ugly*, there's a pan that got you into doing the *Cinefuge* stuff…

John Porter
Yeah, my *Cinefuge* film is basically inspired by a specific scene in *The Good, the Bad and The Ugly* where the camera is spinning around like that and the background is completely blurred. It became abstract and I thought, "Oh wow, abstract image in a commercial movie, I didn't know you could do that!"

Jaap Pieters
Is that the scene in the cemetery? Is that the scene in the graveyard?

John Porter
Yeah.

Jaap Pieters
Ah, yeah, I remember that.

John Porter
And again, over-the-top music, with trumpets blaring!

Chris Kennedy
So it was a technical detail.

John Porter
Yeah. It's interesting to think of this over-the-top musical with this sort of abstract image. It felt incongruous.

Jaap Pieters
Yeah, music has always felt like the refuge place for me to be. There I could exist. In music.

Chris Kennedy
You documented the music scene a bit more with pictures of punks and stuff like that. Or was that just a particular project?

Jaap Pieters
Ah, the film project was based on that photo book that existed, yeah. But no, I was not able to photograph punks because I had long hair. And I'd been threatened several times. Punks with chains running after me in a park, I was on a bike, and they…
    I mean the early punk things, I loved a lot. I saw the first punk concert of the Sex Pistols in Amsterdam. I did see that. January '77. And I saw a lot of those bands when it was still not such an issue. At the first concert it

was never really an issue that there was a hippy watching their music. Listening to their music. Jumping around crazy like them. But as soon as it became fashionable they had all these other idiots that thought they were more punk than any other punk and they liked beating up people. Oh, there was always this stupid side of them.
John Porter
It reminds me of something I always remember Bruce Elder saying. He was actually one of my teachers at Ryerson. He was one of these teachers who wouldn't take super 8 seriously. I remember he was talking about The Funnel once and describing super 8 as punk. "Oh, those are just punk films." Heh heh. But they weren't...

Jaap Pieters
Yeah, yeah, yeah.

John Porter
There was nothing punky about the films we were making at all.

Jaap Pieters
No, but there is something that is very much like punk music. That's the way I've described it a couple of times. Punk was a necessity after rock music got really so thick and dense and huge and massive that you hardly could breathe any more and punk was a necessity to break through that. And their main thing was do-it-yourself. You can't play. Doesn't matter. Play. You can't play any note, any chord. Doesn't matter. You play. And that was what film, what filmmaking with super 8, was for me. You can do it yourself. Just shoot.

John Porter
Yup. And super 8 sort of blossomed at the same time as

punk music because super 8 sound was introduced in
1975. And that's when people really started thinking about
shooting super 8 more. When the cameras became better,
more sophisticated, and you could shoot with sound.

Jaap Pieters

I didn't even know that. But this whole punk attitude was
to me always important in the filmmaking. And super 8
filmmaking itself, as an act, has this same type of attitude.

John Porter

Yeah, so I guess Bruce was right. But he was putting it
down for that reason.

Jaap Pieters

Yeah, right. That's why punks called themselves punks.
But there is another subject that I think is interesting: the
whole idea of subculture and underground. That's another
thing I liked about Warhol. Once, when he was asked if he
would prefer to be called an underground filmmaker, he
said, "Well, who wants to be underground? Who wants to
be under the ground?" We all want our films to be seen.
We don't want to be underground.

I loved that as a reaction because the underground
always gives you this feel of yes, we are small, we are little,

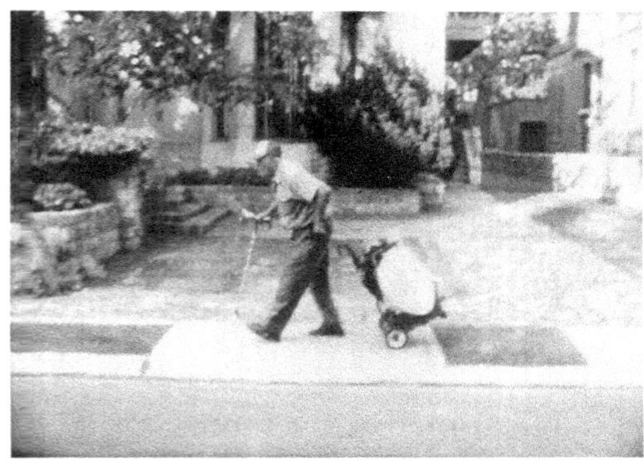

Blade Sharpener
John Porter. 1998

and we are very special and exclusive and they don't know about it. And that's always something that I never really fully understood. I mean of course you do things that people don't attend massively. Yeah, that's true. But seeing it as some kind of specialty that you do underground and therefore it is better—that I always felt uneasy with. It's not better because you are underground. I mean, you either make things or you make bad things and you have bad things in the underground and good things in the underground, but I love going to an opera. I really like going to operas. Mainly twentieth century operas. But yeah, I would go to the opera every month if I would have the money. That's only the question of money.

That level of music is to me—I can't divide it, like I can't divide anything, actually. It's all part of existing and I don't want to make those choices.

John Porter
Well there's an aspect of underground, which is by choice. I often refer to the underground cinemas like CineCycle and Trash Palace as underground cinemas. They have to be underground to a degree because they are illegal. You know they're not zoned for public assembly, so called, and they're selling alcohol often illegally, so they're by choice pretty much not very visible. You have to be careful about getting too much over ground because then you have to start complying with all these laws.

Jaap Pieters
Yeah, right.

…

John Porter
How do you feel about scratches? This is what I get asked

all the time because I'm showing my originals.

Jaap Pieters
Well, I'm variable about it. I mean that scratch on *The Weight*—the film with the pumpkin—I really don't like as it is mostly in the face. And I'm only hoping that the original doesn't have that scratch. I don't know. I don't know where it came on. I don't remember.

John Porter
Oh, that's interesting.

Jaap Pieters
It might be possible that the original doesn't have that scratch. And there's this other film. I didn't show it here. I don't know if you saw it. I don't know where I showed it. The one that I shot in the mountains in Switzerland?

Chris Kennedy
No, you didn't show it here.

Jaap Pieters
It was chosen to be in the festival in Zurich, in their competition. I think it was the only super 8 in that edition of the festival and then they had a Bauer projector and I had mine. And they said, "Ah, Jaap Pieters, don't bother to take the projector out. We've got ours set up already and you can use it."

And then their projector really zig-zagged through about two or three meters of the whole film and you still see it. Also this other film, that very short one, *The Furious with Bottle and Can*. It really was very badly damaged. None of your films have ever been really damaged?

John Porter
No, there's been some damage, but as I say again, I'm very
careful about projecting them. I clean the projector and
clean the films and I project them myself.

In *Toy Catalogue* there's one scene where there's
some sprocket damage and I've left it in. Because its an
important scene and the sprocket damage only goes on
for five seconds, so I don't let that bother me. Some of
those old prints that I made in the eighties that I've shown
a lot—they've got some scratches. That's the only reason,
that I prefer when possible to show the originals and not
the print.

Chris Kennedy
Well, but what do you think about scratches, then?

John Porter
Well, I'd rather not have them be there, especially the
more noticeable they are. Like one down the center of the
film. But then there are other films that are just sort of
totally chaotic and in some ways even scratches help them
even more.

Jaap Pieters
Yeah, I recognize that. And the scratches that are on that
particular copy of *Radio Man and the Candle Woman*
I don't even care much about. They're really even side
scratches. I mean, the film has been shown, so...

I'm always very careful with the projection. I mean
I mostly project myself, almost always, unless I don't
know the projector. But, I mostly have my own projector.
In Canada it was not possible to bring my projector.

John Porter
I wanted to ask you more about your projecting style.

You don't gang your films up on one reel. They're all on separate reels. I have no problems with ganging my films up although I like the sort of home movie feel of having separate reels and talking while you're changing reels.

When I project, like I say sometime I gang them up, because I like to fit in 60 minutes of running time within a 90-minute evening. That's another reason why I like to talk over the films. Saves time from talking between films, you know.

Jaap Pieters

Well, my show is in general very fast and I always rewind, but it's never a problem because the rewinding with the Bauer is done extremely quickly. I can rewind them between 30 and 40 seconds and then a new film is on. I tell the story and some times there's applause, sometimes not. I tell the anecdote and mostly the next film is ready but I'm still talking.

John Porter

Did you meet Peggy Ann Berton last night? I think she's an amazing filmmaker. She has some real similarities to both you and I but real differences, too. In fact, I would say, in presentation style, she's sort of halfway between you and I. She does her own projecting, she rewinds be-

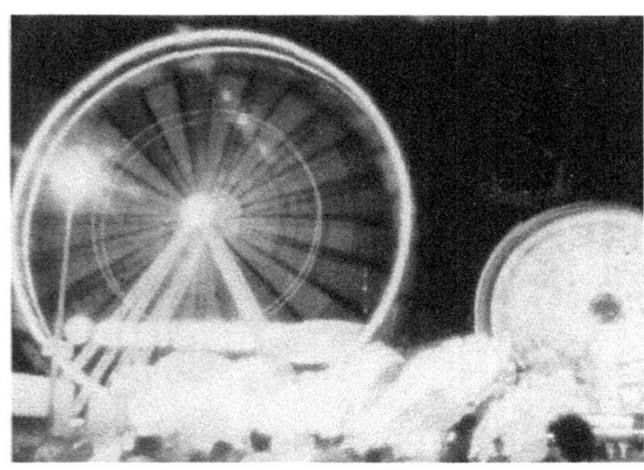

Amusement Park
John Porter. 1979

tween each film and the similarities she has with me but not you is she talks over the films. She calls them *Super 8 Beat Soliloquies* and she has a real sort of you know, beat, Jack Kerouac mentality. She'll talk as she's showing the films. She'll show some slow motion, like 6 frames per second, and she changes the speed when she gets to a scene she wants to be shorter. Sometimes the films aren't even directly related to what she's talking about she'll be telling some story about when she went to New York and the film will be of some tree or something like that. And the stories are really good they're sort of political and funny and outrageous.

She has a really unique style. And also she's a real smoker and drinker and before when smoking was allowed in bars, that was part of her show. She'd have the little projector there and an ash tray full of butts and ashes and a couple of beers on the go. It was fantastic. It would be great if you could see one of her shows. She's shown in that room—the Art Bar at the Gladstone Hotel.

Chris Kennedy

There's something about super 8 that really allows for intimacy. That seems to be the forefront of what your performance aspect is—the intimacy of the performance.

John Porter

I think part of that is technical, is because the projectors aren't very bright so you can't get a big image. It's really better in small rooms, a small image.

Jaap Pieters

Then there's the other Elmo, that Daïchi Saito brought to Detroit.

John Porter
Yeah, that's a Xenon lamp.

Jaap Pieters
That was a Xenon lamp and that has a beautiful lens as
well. It really made a huge image in Detroit. Now he pre-
ferred the smaller lens with the smaller image but I said,
well, I want it big. And to me it looked great. I was standing almost in the screen, together with the film *Willem I,
Willem II, Willem III*. I was about this size and this was
the head of Willem. And I saw some of those photographs
of that and it really looked great.

John Porter
We were talking about size, I usually prefer a smaller image, because then it's bright. But a lot of audience people
want to see a big image. But if you want to see a good film,
it needs to be brighter.

Jaap Pieters
Yeah, but we found a size that that it still had enough
brightness and I think, in general, my films are quite
bright, so with that particular lens Daïchi had it was really
big and still bright. We didn't blow it up to the largest size
that the lens could do. It was a zoom lens.

John Porter
And how do you feel about projecting booths as opposed
to the projector in the room with the audience?

Jaap Pieters
I don't like it.

John Porter
You don't like what?

Jaap Pieters

I don't like the booths.

John Porter

Yeah, me neither. The projector's part of the show and I think its part of the intimacy too you're talking about with super 8.

Jaap Pieters

I don't like the booths but sometimes you have no choice.

John Porter

Yeah, its a real disconnect. The worst booths are the ones to get up there you have to go out the door down the hall up the stairs. At The Funnel we had a booth but you could sort of stick you head out from the booth and hear the theatre, you know it was that close. It's like that at Cine-Cycle, too.

Jaap Pieters

The booth in Montréal at the Segal is a bit like that you can very easily just stick out your head, but then, some-how it really didn't work. I thought it was a very beautiful show, just like yesterday; there are so many people who re-mained for the question and answers as well. In Montréal nobody left. There were 33 people and they all remained until we were kicked out because we were sitting there ready to talk there for another hour. Yeah, it was pretty amazing.

John Porter

And what was the Detroit venue like? Wasn't that a com-mercial cinema?

Jaap Pieters

Well, it was big. I wouldn't call it commercial. It's a very huge 1200 seat theatre and part of the Detroit Institute of Arts. Completely art deco, gold all over. When I got into the building I saw the entrance hall and then there was another hall and then before we went into that I though, "wow, this is amazing." I really was very pleased that I could show my films there. The place is so incredible. I mean I love art deco.

John Porter

Were you taking pictures?

Jaap Pieters

Well, no because I did not have my own camera. I mean. I have one camera and it has a flash but the lens is broke, so...

John Porter

A flash wouldn't work in a big room like that anyway.

Jaap Pieters

No, but I couldn't take pictures. I was preparing. I still had a lot of things to do and then this guy—this volunteer guy—I asked him to take a lot of pictures and he promised me a CD but he never showed up at the festival again. So he took a lot and I hope he still has them. And I hope I still can get them.

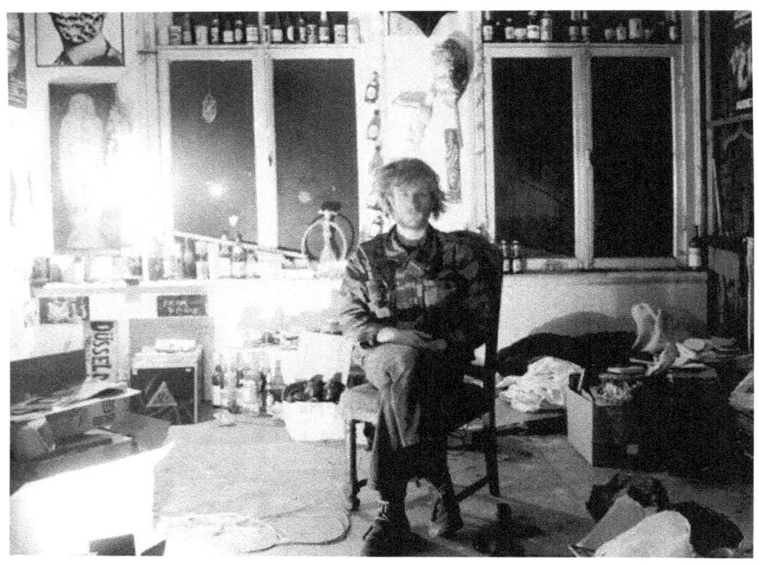

Jaap Pieters, affectionately nicknamed *The Eye of Amsterdam*, started filmmaking in the early 1980s. Since then, he has made hundreds of super 8 films and taken thousands of photographs. He started touring his films in 1997 and has since shown his films extensively in Europe, becoming a notable fixture of the International Film Festival Rotterdam and the active microcinema and festival scene. In 2011 he had his first North American tour of his films. The EYE Film Institute Netherlands has blown up many of his films to 35mm for preservation purposes and projection prints of those films are available through them (www.eyefilm.nl/) or through Light Cone in Paris (http://lightcone.org). He was the subject of four documentaries, most recently: *Jaap Pieters portret* (2005) by Fred Pelon and *The Universe of Jaap Pieters* (2015) by Barbara den Uyl.

His website http://jaappieters.com documents his active agenda, with numerous screenings throughout the year.

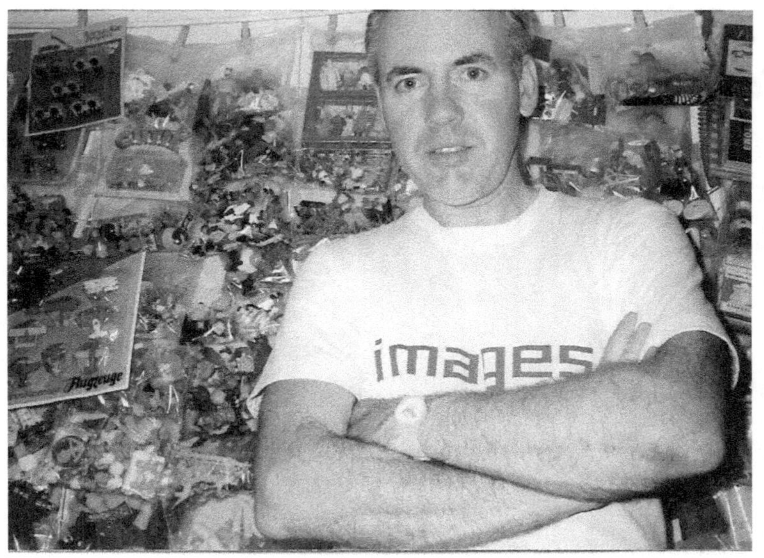

John Porter has been making films since 1968. He has made over three hundred super 8 films. He has been active in the Toronto film community since the 1970s, notably as a member of *The Funnel Experimental Film Theatre* that ran from 1977-1989 and of *Pleasure Dome* (founded 1989) and *CineCycle Underground Cinema* (founded 1991). He has been Toronto's most ardent film historian, documenting the fringe film scene with his photography. Some of this photography will be published in the forthcoming book *Documentary Portraits from Toronto and Other Alternative Film Scenes, 1978-2014*. An extensive interview with him was published in Scott Mac-Donald's *A Critical Cinema 3: Interviews with Independent Filmmakers* (University of California Press, 1998).

John Porter maintains www.super8porter.ca, which is an excellent online resource for more information on his work and on the Toronto film scene in general. John Porter self-distributes his films and can be reached via that website.

Chris Kennedy is a Toronto based writer, film-maker, and film programmer. He is the Executive Director of the Liaison of Independent Filmmakers of Toronto. His website is www.theworldviewed.com

Published 2015
Toronto Canada